LEEWAY & ADVENT

LEEWAY & ADVENT

Poems by

Louis Gallo

Cover design by Shay Culligan

ISBN: 978-1-954353-21-3

Kelsay Books
502 South 1040 East, A-119
American Fork, Utah, 84003

for Cat, Claire & Madeleine, as always

Acknowledgments

North of Oxford Literary Magazine: "*Tree*"; *Utopia Science Fiction Magazine:* " Mind," "Bell's Theorem," "Disorder," "Brain Cells"; *Artemis Literary Journal:* "The Goddess Descends"; *The Lake* [British poetry journal]: "*I started a joke*"; *The MacGuffin:* "Praying Mantises"; *Glass: A Journal of Poetry:* "Mercy"; *Aperion Review:* "Rockwell's America"; *Rattle*: "Fairy Tale"; *Boston Poetry Magazine: "Outing"; Scarlet Leaf Review:* "The Old House"; *Clapboard House:* "Porn Stars"; *The Voices Project:* "Proteus"; *MisfitMagazine:* "Raining Ants"; *Offcourse Literary Journal:* Ah!" "The Treason of Punctuation"; *Here Comes Everybody* (Silhouette Press, Britain): "The Night I Was Saved, Almost"; *North of Oxford Literary Magazine:* "Getting Wasted with Elpenor"; *Xavier Review:* "Fool Such As I"; *Adelaide Literary Magazine:* "In the Waiting Room as My Child Undergoes Surgery"; *River Poets Journal:* "All in a Night's Work"; *Teaching as a Human Experience* (Cambridge Scholar's Publishing): "Logos"; *Segue 9:* "Kindergarten Poem"; *Poetry Pacific:* "Our Daily Bread"; *Pennsylvania Literary Journal:* "Reading Baudelaire," The Dialectic of High and Low," "Audubon in New Orleans, 1821," "Abelard and Heloise," "Tarot: the Fool," "Dying to Live"; *The Rain, the Party and Disaster:* "Intimations of Mortality"

Contents

I.

Praying Mantises   15
Tree   17
Mercy   18
Rockwell's America   19
Old Photos   20
Brain Cells   21
Whittling Time   22
Leeway   23
Squirrel   24
Mind   25
Logos   26
Fairy Tale   27
One Birthday or Another   28
One Day   29
Proteus   30
Bell's Theorem   32
The Old House   33
Our Daily Bread   35
Audubon in New Orleans, 1821   36
The Dialectic of High and Low   38
Reading Baudelaire   39

II.

Abelard and Heloise   43
Outing   44
Perspective   45
Poet   46
Religion   47
The Hunger of Time   48
The Map Is Not the Territory   49
Mind Geography   50

The Emperor   51
That Point to Which it has Come and Will Always
    Come   52
Supermarket   53
Mulberries   55
Absalom: Prodigal Son   56
Amenities   57
Ah!   58

III.

Agenbite of Inwit   61
I Started a Joke   62
Copyediting   63
Hell is Other People   64
Chaos   65
Clinging Vine   66
In the Waiting Room as My Child Undergoes
    Surgery   67
Family Reunion   69
Missing   70
To All the Music We Shall Never Hear   71
Intimations of Mortality   72
The Treason of Punctuation   74
Getting Wasted with Elpenor   76
The Night I Was Saved, Almost   77
Tarot: The Fool   78
Dying to Live   80
Disorder   82
Etruscans   83
Raining Ants   84
Fool Such as I   85

IV.

Morning Walk by the River   91
Sweet Sorrow   92
Porn Stars   94
Mayday, or, Prayer to Bob Villa   96
Stuffed Artichokes   97
Words   99
Snow   101
Just a Note   102
Secret   103
Rife with Passage   104
Snapshot of Pablo Neruda   105
All in a Night's Work   106
Kindergarten Poem   109

V. Advent

Dec 1:   115
Dec 2:   116
Dec 3:   117
Dec 4:   118
Dec 5:   119
Dec 6:   120
Dec 7:   121
Dec 8:   122
Dec 9:   123
Dec 10:   124
Dec 11:   125
Dec 12:   126
Dec 13:   127
Dec 14:   128
Dec 15:   129
Dec 16:   130

Dec 17:   131
Dec 18:   133
Dec 19:   134
Dec 21:   136
Dec 22:   137
Dec 23:   138
Dec 24:   139
Dec 25:   140

I.

Praying Mantises

At night the stuccoed walls
of the gymnasium rise like ghostly crags.
Mercury vapor from the parking lights
drenches its luminous done.
I have come for the spectacle,
the mantises, millions of them,
paralyzed witnesses who will stay
two or three days, then disappear.
My tires crushed dozens as I parked.
I destroy them when I seek a place
to stand without killing, maiming more.

They don't seem to care
and hardly bother to move or spring.
Nothing disturbs the crazed adoration
of this devout swarm.
They fasten to parking signs, wire fences,
fire hydrants, telephone wires,
but mostly blanket the congenial asphalt.
The hazy, metallic glow of the lights
coats them with an eerie fragility
though doubtless they could gather
in one massive thrust to finish me off.

This is the sixth year they have returned
in a decade. I keep such tally.
They neither feed nor mate,
seem to have no purpose or mission
other than worship—
reason enough to join them.

I sink, face the dome in a small clearing
and imagine it some holy place.
Slowly my hands rise in supplication.
We pray, the throng and I,
in silent, fervid assembly.
I will regret when the wind sweeps
them up like twigs and they vanish again,
leaving me here alone on my knees.

Tree

I am watching men in hard hats and chain saws
amputate limb by limb, before they destroy
the trunk, a most magnificent oak tree
across the street—for no apparent reason.
I have admired this tree for decades, the
tallest in the neighborhood, even the city,
and no doubt hundreds of years old.

It must surely rise over three hundred feet,
though I am not much at guessing distance.
It's wide as a massive ziggurat, and who knows
how deeply its roots burrow into the earth.
I imagine it reaching into the sky to touch
Orion, that it is in fact a sublunary Orion
itself, an Orion being butchered
for no reason, for no reason, for no reason.
This is the way it goes with the sacred.

Mercy

Don't probe fluorescence
or polymer or the crowded aisles
of Legget's Department Store
after Labor Day.
Get out of Colorado.
Avoid Mecca and Stonehenge.
Mercy is a loner, shy and frugal.

Look to the empty stairwell
between stories, back alleys,
lonely boiler rooms
or dusty attics.
Here it will come,
meek as doves, fire on its tongue.
Squeeze into a crawl space
and keep quiet.
Surrender the one mean bone
in your body.

Rockwell's America

Empty bottles of Pepto-Bismol
wail like bassoons in every niche.
One of us can only drink
decaffeinated coffee and no tea.
Television programs are off limits,
especially the dire Weather Channel.
We swallow three capsules
of Librium a day.

Nothing is good for us.
Soap scratches our skin. Fruit breaks us out.
Before bed we massage
each other's kidneys with lanolin.
Our physicians advise us to dim the lights.
The children have eerie heartbeats.
They sob in the refrigerator.
We try to keep their fevers down.

Old Photos

They too yearn,
like greedy fingers
plucking tiny stars
from the dark sky's ice,
as if grief,
that stable of the will,
could churn itself
into fragrant cream.
I turn pages
and sip leftover water.
The dog is dead.

Here's Missouri, decades ago,
wife, child, the black cat
and me [understood, invisible],
the duration of a flash,
the house a hive
crumbling at its joints.
And this in Virginia,
a room barren of all
save the voice of a child.

Wave upon wave of foamy time
sweeping us to what still shore?
Forgive me if I pause,
grant me expanse;
nudge me into some polaroid
immune to greening,
Ultimate Crunch
and Year of the Mineral.

Brain Cells

I.

We lose one hundred thousand a day
after age thirty, and surely there are only
so many to lose. But what if the number
were infinite. Losing so many would matter
about as much as the evaporation of a drop
of rain. Does the infinite die with the finite?
Would there be a grand diaspora of your
brain cells throughout the cosmic hotel?
Specks of your imagination free-floating
everywhere, near Alpha Centauri, between
the Dipper's stars, out at the rim of
the known universe (woe unto those
wayward saboteurs who choose hovels
of dark matter in which to burrow).

II.

But fear not. The infinite has no sway
this side of the Mason-Dixon. Let us focus,
then, upon that final and no doubt quivering
cell about to vanish into the spiritual muck
along with all the other tenants of your once
chateau of a brain. Let that last cell throb
with an image of her lips, slightly moist
and parted with a modest slice of snow owl
teeth bordering the upper, lips bee-stung
with subtle vertical ridges that fade
with a smile . . . and let it, if not asking
too much, recall my own lips meeting them
as all four linger for that volt of a moment.

Whittling Time

The old man rubs the thumb and forefinger
of his right hand against the thumb of his left,
methodically, in deft precision.
We who expect to learn something
from this otherwise worthless prop whose clothes
have begun to leak into his skin,
who, suffused in a cloudy patina of vino,
never shifts his legs, never bathes,
has become no more nor less than a knick-knack
upon our shelves, haunting our holidays
and parlor at tv time
(we can hardly define ourselves without reference
to the old man, a weightless anchor
to our gliding across the surface
of some green lagoon, this gargoyle of genealogy,
ancestral shrine of our devotion) . . .
we flick ashes off our wrists as the half dead past,
inert hangnail of obligation clings, snags us roughly,
and not without pain, in the coarse fabric of passage.

Leeway

that little bit of stretch
between the shadow and the monolith,
the flexion between pursed lips
and a kiss, the tilt of a windmill,
the elastic margin in your otherwise
tedious precision. . .
the lifespan flitting between
two steel jaws at both ends

Squirrel

It dashed in front of my tires
so fast I had time only to grasp
the whole thing passing
out of my hands—

and in the rear view,
the twitches, convulsions
as if in ecstasy,
and me, pulling over
to puke.

Mind

Drunk on its own salty ions,
the mind surges toward truth;
it churns with desire
then abates—meek fingers
that lap but finally lose the shore,
evaporate in the sun.
Locked in its rigid basin,
the mind roams,
but truth farther,
a blind sea bird soaring
beyond itself.

Logos

I tell students they must also
consider the beauty of certain words
not in terms of meaning alone
but as sound qua sound,
that is, as music.

Here, three words that mean
the same thing in different languages:
Casa, maison, house.
Who likes the sound of *casa* best?
Maybe a hand from way back, row six.

How about *house?*
No hands from any row ever.
Maison? Ninety-nine percent every time.
French, it's always French.

And then I tell them about *deliquescence.*

Fairy Tale

Once upon a time
there was no time.

The minutes were monsters
sewn out of hatred.

They tear the young princess
from the house of her father.

She grows up a stranger,
he falls into darkness.

A lord without light,
he prays that this story

will end without ending
or end right.

One Birthday or Another

I remember only
the buzzing fan
purr steadily
as it lulled us
into buttery sleep,
my birthday,
a sesame seed
swept off with
that minor breeze.

One Day

You will not be there to tell them
goodbye

You will have become the silent
embodiment of goodbye

And finally the disembodiment

Proteus

You've heard of me from Classics 101.
A sea god of turbulent shapeshifting.
What they didn't tell you
is that you, composed of mostly brine,
are me. That ego of yours, which seeks
the stolidity of an anchor, steers
you wrong, makes you think you're
carved in stone, a regular Doric column.

Who were you yesterday? I was Ajax,
slaughtering imaginary sheep as I slept.
Sweet Sally over there, she found snakes
in her hair and turned Joey to granite
until she got sweet again and jellied
him down—oh, like a sheep he bleated,
pecked her sneakers. And you, Father,
your metamorphosis the grandest
along with everyone else now dust-
grained, granulated, scatter-strewn.
How we blend and ooze, osmosify, (is this a word?)
one day Chuck the clunk, the next,
Balthazar the wise.

And as I sit
on a stool in this diner waiting for
a plate of scrambled eggs I watch
the waitress, beautiful Nausicaä,
alchemize into Sweet Sally with snakes
for hair when she burns her finger
on a hot skillet. She sucks out the heat,
feels better, is Nausicaä again
and I am sea-weeded, crusty Ulysses
washed up by the ocean once more
onto her dainty shore
like a chunk of worm-holed driftwood.

Bell's Theorem

Two particles once connected
on this side of the universe,
will, when separated by trillions
of light years, respond instantly
to the same itch, the sudden jab,
the scent of roses.
And they will respond identically.
Faster than light.
As if geography doesn't count.

Everything is connected,
in love, kissing, space and time,
illusion . . . we're all married.
If one of us dies on this side,
the other, far away, will croak.
Einstein detested the idea
but could not defeat
its mathematical elegance.

Surely this implies god,
and if not god,
something like god.
Time to break out
the champagne,
ring in all time
as that other god
or whatever,
way out yonder,
sniffs the evanescence.

The Old House

for Cathy

1.

We take the long way so our baby can see
October fire in the trees. You hated the house
When we lived there and so did I.
I sensed my other child in every room,
Heard her call my name long after she was gone.
You sensed traces of another woman.
Yet what a time we had that year we stayed
Waiting for the sale. We sat outside in snow
To gaze at stars crisp as sugar.
I felt blood course through your hand
As I held it in silent benediction–
The hours we spent exploring each other's
Flesh despite ghosts and fear.
It has been five years and now safe enough
To visit. It seems small, you exclaim,
As we pass–and dingy, I add, who would paint
A house the color of skin?
Yet we can't stop looking, turn the car,
Circle the block. It's just another house,
I sigh and shift my eyes to the road for good.

II.

When we stop at McDonald's
I pluck an apple from a tree next to the parking lot
And prop it on the dashboard. You offer to drive home
To our new town. I lie back with Claire
Who, strapped in her car seat, can't stop smiling.
She will never know this place;
I will never hear her call from desolate rooms.
I mourn that other daughter as our baby curls
Her tiny fingers around my thumb.
We stop again for roadside cider.
I watch you walk toward a row of jugs
And choose one. You look so beautiful
I want to sing out. We are done with history
For a while and speed out of the past.
I reach over your seat for the apple
But you fling it out of the window.
I watch that last token of remembrance
Careen backward, fall, shatter to bits
On the interstate.

Our Daily Bread

Wheatfields may be beautiful in their way
Though one could mistake them for weird grass
Run amuck, yet some primitive genius thought,
Hmmm, I can make bread out of this stuff.
He was probably a nerd, outcasted by his
Mighty, manly fellow hunters—couldn't hunt
Worth a damn—but the bread caught on and
Issued in civilization and usurped the hunters
Who soon caved in to the farmers.

No one knows that genius's name or when
His eureka eurekaed—not as with Guttenberg's
Printing press or Edison's light bulb or Eli Whitney
Or Henry Ford. He remains an anonymous
Visionary, long gone, though the bread lives on.
I like to think also that he sang poems (no writing
Then) to his children about bread, lyrics, maybe odes,
Since the process alchemizes one thing into another
The way mere words transmute into beautiful artifacts
About love and death and time and every now and then
Bread.
        So I celebrate that failed hunter, that lone
Anonym who first separated the wheat from the chaff.

Audubon in New Orleans, 1821

I shall burn my house with the rising dawn,
And leave but the ashes and smoke behind . . .
    —Robert Penn Warren, *Audubon: A Vision*

this long after Saint-Dominique and Nantes, long after
the flute and violin, dancing and riding, long after
his dashing repute as life of the party, failing
as a naval office and the bout with yellow fever in New York,
long after marriage in Kentucky and meeting Daniel Boone,
though he had already declared his affinity with birds
and his admiration for native Americans, long after
American citizenship, bankruptcy and incarceration
for debt, some thirty years before his death . . .

he complains about heat and mosquitoes, misses
his wife, hates the citron hue of Creoles, notices
women eyeing him up (for he is a handsome man)
spots an alligator by Lake Pontchartrain, suffers
headaches, impoverished, paints portraits for cash,
suffers a filthy landlady in his room on Barracks
near Royal, cries misery, grumbles that no one
appreciates his work despite lavish praise in London,
wishes he had never left Natchez, will eventually plunge
into dementia . . .

so what are we to make of an artist who kills
the specimens he loves in order to sketch them
with precision, and the larger question does not every artist
in effect "kill" his subjects, his models, bathe them
in formaldehyde, render them fossilized for the sake
of creating static, immobile and lifeless drafts
of a sketch, a poem, a novel, a sculpture, a symphony?
I'm thinking of those frozen figures on the Grecian Urn
and the paralyzed perfection of Byzantium,
the silent, elongated rage of Shostakovich.
must we embalm to survive forever?

we frolic and picnic now in a park named after him,
the park, a former indigo and sugar cane plantation
(owned by Etienne de Boré, first mayor of New Orleans)
while he lies buried in the Trinity Church Cemetery
in ever humming Manhattan.

The Dialectic of High and Low

Say I'm the pawn that toppled the king
on some chessboard or the peasant who leered
at the queen as she passed in her carriage
of lacquer and filigree, I executed
duly of course for lascivious treason . . .
say anything you want, the metrics
always remain the same, the ups &
downs, rising and sinking like pistons
in an eternal engine of disequilibrium.

Our socks have holes, our collars stained,
as we skulk on the outskirts of the Museum
of Splendid Remains, where they've propped up
the glistening anatomies of that defunct king
and his queen, sullied by my sordid glance—
And I? They sank my ashes into the Bog
of the Forgotten—a ghastly place
teeming with the remnants of renegades.
What a slop of ruin and desolation!

And so the dialectic clashes and unfolds
as it has always clashed and unfolded . . .
but with new players who are replicants
of previous and future players, winning
and losing forever, and, though some claim
that the last shall be the first and the first
never the last, we all wind up in a catacomb
of sorts, pyramids or peat bogs. It all
depends on how sweetly one can sing, whatever
and wherever the architecture, steeple or dungeon.

Reading Baudelaire

whereupon I slammed shut the book
hurled that clock against a wall
and sped out the door
radioactive words etched in my brain
they burn I burn
(but that's Sappho)

because I couldn't take it
couldn't take it
monstrous time, bestial your jaws
saw-toothed, ratcheted

the sweet past, a dream
of opulence, lace curtains,
her cobalt bowl on the table
bulging with wet grapes
and figs

souviens-toi! prodigue! esto memor

to remember is all
to remember the past
creates the past
to remember her, her lips
and golden wheat hair
and the kiss frozen in time

excavate, archaeologist
of nostalgia, of desire . . .
the future has diminished,
the smashed clock still ticks
sinister fleurs, fleurs du mal

II.

Abelard and Heloise

How can I describe that moment when the uncle and hired thugs broke into my chamber and bereft me of the very vessel by which I conjoined my love for God and Heloise at once other than to say that an instant of Hell deposed me forever and that this hell in which I now reside is nothing in compare? And our child, Astrolabe, what is to become of . . .?

Canon Fulbert, the uncle, loved his niece perhaps more than did I, though how can that be since I loved her blasphemously, more than God. She was twenty years younger than I, the most cultured and beautiful woman in all Europe, she, winding up in a nunnery, not by choice. And her painful letters to me, rebuking me for giving her up, for not eloping into the wilds?

Why am I compelled to read them again and again? As if one supreme torture were not enough. Sic et Non. I cast philosophic questions to the wind. I knew her, I knew the only real passion there is, and I yearn for it again and will yearn eternally though one of my torments here is reliving the severing of my manhood repeatedly. These repeats do not come close in severity to the original. You can never reenact the Ur-moment except in diluted ritual.

All in all, to have known her redeems me. What other man can claim as much? And for this I thank the God who cast me out, I thank the Canon for castrating me, and I thank Hell for suffering me to remember.

Outing

We took a wrong turn off US 741
and found ourselves on a mud road
no American car could maneuver.
After a dreary hour of country scenes—
how many country scenes can there be?—
we came upon an obstacle, a cow,
lodged in the middle of the path
like a living boulder.
Of course, it was the little foreign convertible
out of place, an event for the cow.
At the time, though,
behind some green Missouri hills,
an autumn sun sinking fast,
we declared a state of emergency.

The horn did no good.
The cow reeled her head
and stared serenely at the blind swash
of red, as if to say, get lost.
I feared trying to pass.
I don't know the ways of cows.
Do they charge like bulls
at the sight of red?
Couldn't take the chance
so I backed up the car
for what seemed miles
until we came to a clearing
and could swing around.

Back on the American highway
we laughed at the encounter
and agreed we had experienced
experience at last.

Perspective

That squirrel outside my window
scampering up the hemlock tree
will not complain, as would I,
the ascent too prodigious, too
difficult, and, besides, my claws,
no longer in their prime,
I who have assaulted this hemlock
so many times, day in day out,
so oft I long to climb another tree
or at least explore another patch
of ground where I might see,
from inside out, some creature
mounting a different tree,
aromatic, eucalyptical, that charges
through the sense like voltage . . .
and I would say: that something
outside my window, scampering
up the mystic tree, will not complain,
as would he, peering from another
window, at me

Poet

Far down the arid valley
he hears the wee clinks
and chirps of those blind
to the great hulk of black rock
steepling above them
who clink chirp cheep clink
indignantly, who see only
a smudge of darkness
but sometimes dream
of screams whirl winding
from some obscurity
alien to their minds, hearts
what they hate
and think they might fear
and denounce

while aloft he ladles
their chirps and clinks
into a single grace note
too faint to survive

Religion

above three burning bushes,
below a misty aluminum sky,
stationed, a frozen arpeggio,
upon staggered phone lines
taut between cross-shaped poles,
a congregation of sparrows
await the doxology

The Hunger of Time

In a dream, Time came to me
a grizzled, ruined old man
with beard of smoking straw.
"I never get enough of myself,"
he moaned, "I can't keep up."

Foolish I pitied the wretch
and offered him a portion
of my wristwatch.

He glanced with disdain, spat
out an hourglass and swatted
at the pure geometry of space.

The Map Is Not the Territory

If Einstein is right about the continuum
of space and time (and he is)
then as your years glide by
you no longer have the entire planet
to explore and fecundate
like some giddy Magellan—
provided you don't get slain
on your journey—

no, your footage shrinks,
down from continents
to some Ohio then some segment
of Ohio
and pretty soon your territory
amounts to a six-foot patch
which you can sightsee
forever

Mind Geography

there are desolate places where
nothing happens, an inky miasma,
cold and lifeless, boundless catacombs
though sometimes you find yourself
sprawled in Acapulco, a platter
of guava and grapes on your table,
the girls twirling and laughing,
one picking a mandolin, another
swinging hoops of fire

and you, traveler, wish you could stay
but the road map comes alive
and you're on it in your DeSoto,
headed for the Industrial Canal
where you sink for a while
then lurch up for swigs of oxygen
and pump gas into the vehicle
which carries you where it wants,
when it wants . . . all over the terrain

so don't ever get used to where
you are because you're never there
for long

The Emperor

The bones of the middle-class clack
with trepidation. They tiptoe
across that tightrope Kierkegaard
strung over the abyss. Their
children, pale and ghostly, pray
over candles as the dead
accumulate. The Emperor mandates
their extinction as an historical
category. Meanwhile, the peasants
blast "Turkey in the Straw" in a
parking lot where they swig
Thunderbird and devour mac & cheese,
chunks of watermelon and sugar rolls.
They thank the Emperor
for such largesse. They always get by
except for the ones who disappear.
The Emperor loves his people
and drowns them with mercy
at His whim.

That Point to Which it has Come and Will Always Come

But no return to what? That initial oblivion,
before the avalanche of birth, where or what
was that? When I think of the countless billions,
not merely people but also the animals,
from the best dog you ever had to some sac
of protoplasm living under a rock,
everyone, from the Ice Man who slipped
into a ravine and froze to death five thousand
years ago, Lucy Mother of us all peering
through tall grasses of the savannah,
the greats, Homer, Alexander, Mozart,
those forgotten, the billions forgotten,
those massacred in senseless wars, those
drowned in floods, torched by fires,
ransacked by disease, loss, poverty, grief,
those extinguished at birth, the children
with bald heads of St. Jude's, those mangled
in accidents, those swindled by malefactors,
those who never had a chance, those who did
have a chance, that puppy Blackie I once had
who died of heartworm only four months old,
the woodpecker who visits my pine tree
every afternoon, the insects it devours,
the billions, all racing toward that point,
that hallucinatory, horrific point, which
when I think upon, when I put my finger on,
when I occasionally see the point, seize it
choke on it, grasp it as nothing at all,
no point, nothing, *nada y pues,* nothing,
no point, the empty howl of nothing,
the derangement, that little pup I loved.

Supermarket

The woman in carmine shorts
stares at bins of flesh,
muscle, brain and bone
and I stare at her.
She adjusts the straps
of her brassiere
and turns from Meat
with a look
of sudden revulsion.

She pushes her basket
towards Produce
and I watch her long fingers
fondle squash and radishes
still wet from rinsing.
I place my purchases
on a scale, deposit them
in clean plastic bags.

As usual, I am frugal
and avoid what may spoil.
I part ways with the woman
at Dairy,
pay for my load and step
into a pristine asphalt lot.
Streaks of sweat
inch down my rib case.

As I pull out
the air conditioner
blasting scorched air,
she emerges from the store
cradling a watermelon
caked with mud, swollen,
fresh from the fields.
Always babies, I think,
though what we see
in rear-view mirrors
is always too late.

Mulberries

Each day, as they bloom, I pluck a mulberry
from our tree and chew it up. A modest berry,
lacking distinction and taste, but faithful, profuse.
I have done this every summer for a decade,
turned it into a kind of sacrament. They don't last long.
I'm devouring July, I tell the tree, which listens.
I'm eating time, bit by bit.

The tree thrives in a swirl of lanky pines
near the back driveway. Once the berries go,
it almost seems to disappear. No one, I think,
notices but me and the birds that feast on its fruit
and deposit purple splotches on our windshields.

But I know when the searing cold returns
and long dark days enshroud the mind
I will stand again beside the garbage cans
and tally not only the seasons but the life,
yearning again for the mulberries' inauspicious return.

This is no feast for pleasure, no picnic
or burst of gustatory delight. This is prayer.

I eat prayers; I tell the tree as its unglamorous leaves
flutter with gusts sweeping in from the mountains.
The tree consents, tolerates me in a way
that I, with almost nothing in my hands,
vaguely understand.

Absalom: Prodigal Son

I ransacked my father's house,
I sold his antique Leica for six bucks
because I needed a buzz,
I trashed the mahogany end table he made
with his bare hands because I had to vent,
I stirred his ashes into my own spit
because it felt good,
I traded the gold coin he inherited
from his mother for a jug of honey . . .

but he forgave me.
I have never committed
any crime to surpass
such cruelty.

Amenities

The fringe on a lampshade,
the demitasse cup
with hand-painted dragons,
the butler in the bathroom
of Hilton Splendide
wiping lint from your shoulders
with a whisk broom

cover-ups for shoddy essentials
and too damned expensive

Ah!

Sometimes you've just gotta
leap into the rubbery jello of words
that vat of eelish vocabulary
and get naked, eh?
Oink plop swish clink yowl brrrrrr
zap whah grrrr wham meow 'swounds . . .
because you're one of those monkeys
who will type out all Shakespeare
in infinite time.

III.

Agenbite of Inwit

for Molly

You asked in your poem how it is
that we choke amid such defilement—
our commodification & alienation,
in effect, the "sane" now the most insane
among us, as you dubbed, freaks and outcasts.

I have no answers of course
but I did feel the pain as you read aloud,
the quaver in your otherwise pristine voice,
and I recall asking the same questions
when I was your age and that others,
countless others, throughout the ages,
have also so wondered. Job, why the boils?
Sisyphus, why the boulder?

                Agenbite of Inwit,
which meant remorse in the fourteenth century—
we, those who can feel it, attributing
affliction to some mis-wiring in our own circuitries
rather than bulls-eyeing it toward those
who seize the reins, plunder and impose,
those who ravage, those without souls,
aside from the monstrous tyrants of desire,
language, hormones, anatomy . . .
remorse, guilt—the wages of enlightenment.

I Started a Joke

I wrote a letter to Barry Gibb
offering to take the place
of Robin and Maurice
(may they RIP)
though I can't sing

because I can't stand
to see things end
and I love Robin's
falsetto tremolo
though true you guys
went bad with that
disco caca
but so what?

Everybody writes
a bad poem
every now and then
(like this one),
even Keats . . .
but mostly I hate
things ending
like the Bee Gees
& eventually
the human species,
even the universe . . .
man, I hate that

Copyediting

Helena of Helsinki, a comely
common comma, wore, nevertheless,
the diadem of interruptus, showed
up (like, here) when not needed
or wanted though sometimes
not at all, say, when the waltz in her honor
resounded like confetti at the Ritz
of Herculaneum.

Whereas Vladivostok Vlad, that dashing
yet dastardly dash—
sought to emulate Emily—usually
overdoing it—but occasionally, say,
during a solar eclipse of Sirius
could—if he dared—
get it right or sorta right
and the ensuing silences davened
like dreams—

Hell is Other People

—Sartre

But so is heaven—
thus we're back where we started.
The demons flit among us
as do the angels.
Which shall prevail?

Or perhaps, as a poet once wrote,
you yourself are hell.
What then?

Have some vino, my friend,
and watch the clouds
though remember what
The Preacher warned:
he who regards the clouds
will not reap.
All is vanity.

As if, in the larger scheme,
reaping amounts to nothing:
Tutankhamen

Chaos

turns out there are rules to it,
even formulae,
but if you try to figure them out
you'll go crazy

I once learned in a physics class
that if you knew the momentum
& mass & velocity of a snowball
you could determine how fast
it would melt
when splattered against a wall

oh, and that butterfly effect,
a wing flap in Truth or Consequences
yields an explosion on Saturn

so I'll just render to chaos
what belongs to chaos
and render to order
whatever pertains

somehow entropy figures in
as well as information
but given the eyeblink factor
I'll have a glass of Pinot Noir
now, please, and watch
the dust motes swirling
in a shaft of light

Clinging Vine

I went to clip away the clinging vine
choking our sole rose bush—
it seemed to appear overnight

I found its tenacity impressive
as it launched forth wiry tendrils
that wrapped themselves
in knots around both bush and fence

it took many snips to eradicate it
and in truth I began to feel sorry
for the massacre

was it love or obsession that drove
that fuse so urgently to bind?
was it love or obsession that drove
me to save the roses?

In the Waiting Room as My Child Undergoes Surgery

A small flat screen mounted on the wall
across from where I sit digitally posts
the stages of surgical progression for each
patient. This is, I assume, meant to comfort
those of us here waiting. Below this glowing
bulletin board, a massive television screen—
Kelly Ripa chatting endlessly about nothing.
An aquarium to my right, home for two
bloated goldfish who with lidless eyes
that seem more like fashion buttons than eyes
gaze through the glass. Mostly they float
and so gaze but every so often the larger male
prods the female along her flank and the two
circle their cramped confines. Then they
gaze again beyond that glass impediment at us
and some of us return the gaze
though most of the waiters either nod off
or read magazines or work smartphones.

I had brought along a useful book to help
diminish the gulch of time these affairs
usually consume, but I could not concentrate.
The chosen magazines did not interest me
and Kelly Ripa . . . what is the point of Kelly Ripa?
So I commune with the goldfish, reddish
stationary verbs, either unaware of their captivity
or all too aware with no option but to float
and stare and every so often dart about
in frenzied circles.

And what if the glass shattered? Would they
plummet gladly to their deaths in a cascading wave
of liberation? Or prefer an eternal status quo?
I lift my heavily lidded eyes to the information
screen to learn that my child has now been put
under the knife, her flesh being now opened.
Now. As if at a moment sudden, I know
what the goldfish know.

Family Reunion

The eldest in this room, at 97,
Has lost her reason and her memories;

The youngest, at 3 months,
Has not yet acquired either.

That leaves the rest of us
To suffer both for them.

Missing

I've got the mortar
but not the pestle

at one time I had
the pestle but
not the mortar

something always
missing
something always
amiss

same with the hook
& eye

and the eye itself
missing
what it sees
and seeing
what it misses

To All the Music We Shall Never Hear

Heard a new one, for me, today
driving home from Virginia Tech
after dropping Maddie off
at the bookstore—Ravel's
insane Piano Concerto with
soloist Leonard Bernstein
whose fingers must have set
the instrument on fire.
(And our new "president" wants
to privatize NPR—we all know
what that means. Farewell, arts
of any kind.)
But my concern here is this:

think of all the music we
shall never hear, from the past,
from the future, from even now,
the present—all that we've missed
along the way while busy
changing burnt-out light bulbs,
pumping dinosaur deliquesce
into our hybrids, gathering supplies
at Walmart, Lowes and CVS.

A newly surfaced Beatles song,
a lost but now found Bach motet,
that symphony composed
by the Mozart of the 23rd century.
Imagine all that we've missed,
Hallelujah to what we haven't.
The glass is both half full
and half empty at once.
Cheers. Where's the refill?

Intimations of Mortality

1

Mr. Moose, believe the name or not,
sat on a green three-legged stool
and threw shreds of cardboard boxes
into a fire too hot to understand.
There was I, invisible at every recess,
sulking in the doorway of his great boiler room
wishing I could destroy something too—
not knowing I had.

2

Perhaps I was never a child. It happens.
Why do poets insist that childhood is blessed?
I've only begun to learn to escape my own,
that chaos which for years I mistook as paradise.
I fell into a hole and cracked my teeth on a sewerage pipe.
My sister spilled off a swing and lost consciousness
for hours. Did I swing her too high toward heaven?
And what about the time one of us sliced our feet
to shreds on the floor furnace grill?
It's true, every wound is a small death—
and a frenzy to squeeze life clean.
If only death were an ugly, stinking bird
we could crush with our bare hands.
But death is not a bird.
It is a six-year-old child
bobbing against a tree stump in the fetid canal.

3.

And yet, and yet . . . how sweetly the magnolias flared
on Esplanade Avenue on warm summer evenings,
how splendid our treks to Katz & Besthoff
for malteds and banana splits, our grandmother
trailing in the distance, her purse fat with money.
Nothing ever changed in those days, we lived forever,
we cast no shadows, we glowed on Columbus Street
like radioactive potatoes in the moonlight.

The Treason of Punctuation

What I know I don't know
or
What I know, I don't know
or
What? I know I don't know?

So you've had it with minutia,
the loose button, the errant Band-Aid,
because it confuses you
and induces pain and wastes time,
that dwindling cornucopia,
though deep down you know
(and don't know) that a piece of string
dropped on the mown lawn
can trigger your execution
because some eye mistook
it for the pearls of the empress.

Socrates (he's still alive!)
tells us that wisdom is knowing
you don't know nothing
and I could believe that man
in diapers if only he weren't
so damned old . . . the way
is not the way, never was the way,
never will be the way, so go ahead,
spin in circles on your heels
as you devour that apple
Tantalus can't reach.

There's a wishbone at the bottom
of this bowl of gumbo
but I can't slurp it fast enough
to split the thing in two.
The bowl is always half full.
One lisp, one wayward comma—
and they grab you at the crossroads
to haul you away in a squad car.

Getting Wasted with Elpenor

Pretty bored last night so I decided
to descend to the underworld
hoping to meet the great Achilles
or Agamemnon or, you know, one
of them, even that mad Ajax would do.
Instead I ran into Elpenor sulking
on a lonely, miasmal crossroad.
Seems no one had buried him yet—
remember he's the dopey kid
who got drunk atop Circe's roof
and fell off and broke his neck
(one or two lines in *The Odyssey*).
He'd talk to anybody who drank
the blood, begging, pleading for burial
so his soul could cease its wandering.

Well, I wasn't much help.
Back up on a roof (Circe's again?),
we wound up getting cheap drunk
on Gallo wine—
and once more Elpenor slid off
to still another death, another
broken neck. He looked so sad
as he peered at me from the ground
though I had already explained
that I lacked the power to salvage
either his body or soul. I sang
from my vantage—Ray Charles'
rendition of "Born to Lose,"
never quite deciding who ranks
as the greater losers:
hopeless, broken blokes like Elpenor
or those of us who can't restore them.

The Night I Was Saved, Almost

Last night a band of squeaky, dusty angels
(which at first I mistook for gnats)
arrived with news of my salvation.
Ah, the splendid au revoir at last!
Their leader assured me that no strings
dangled from this package of good fortune.
I passed, he said, a test I didn't take.
How professional, mused I,
and called Marie at once.

Today, I don't know . . .
I'm still here, pale, destitute and sad.
I'd always thought great events happened elsewhere
and in different clothes. But see, the same
trembling hand wipes the same hardened crumbs
off the same cracked table.
And the old sun spits a lethal dawn
right through my windows again.
If anything, I feel worse, more vague
in the throat, and my eyes have moistened
with sentimentality.
No yeast-like rising, no ballyhoo
among the relatives I've notified,
no telegrams, bouquets, no cabs—
and Marie, she's left me for a less righteous man.

Tarot: The Fool

We dined on neon wishbones,
the soup a flamboyant broth
with sugared cucumbers and flan
on that stately terrazzo in Paraguay
or maybe that time in ancient Cathay
when the peasants danced in the street
proclaiming a joyous revolution
as mandarins clattered their teeth
in displeasure.

       You smiled at me with dazzling eyes
as we sipped aperitifs in hammocks
stretched between eucalyptus trees
in Sao Tome,
the ham operator tapping sos
on his brass mechanical key.
Oh, the island birds clamored
in frenzy.

       We bathed and romped naked
in the sulfurous healing springs
of West Virginia where Jefferson
once sought cure. The allure
of blue mountains charmed us
into languid serenity, and we
bathed too in each other's bodies,
liquid in our passion.

Ah, the good life is everywhere
and you are everywhere with me
and life is dolce, dolce,
a mist of confection.
We dreamed our way into
the Major Arcana and yet they still
dub us Zero.

Dying to Live

I tried to kill myself because I wanted to live
—Robert Schumann to his doctor at the madhouse
(as reported by J.D. Landis in Longing)

The doctor could not understand
though Schumann had already confessed
that he went mad every even year
and that he was hearing the persistent
deep throb of a bassoon drowning out
all other sound. Music drove the composer
mad, which he often both lamented
and proudly proclaimed. After all,
audiences of the time found his work
difficult, bizarre and incomprehensible.

And what drives you mad—or I?
Pray it's music or poetry or art
of whatever kind, say, a bronze
by Rodin or the blue bouquets of Monet.
For if it's money or power that drives
us mad, consign us to the dung heap
of capitalism as so described
by the Pope. Or perhaps thwarted
or unrequited love—quite apropos
since love and art consummate
each other on cushions of desire.

Dare we probe the difference
between madness and sanity?

Surely the sane, given the exigencies,
the preposterousness of the universe,
are the maddest of all,
that release, that tango
on the edge of a razor blade—for a
brief but full account of our need
to escape the tyranny of logic,
objectivity, empiricism, "normality."

The mind has fathomless mountains,
said another glorious madman.
One must imagine Sisyphus happy?
Happiness, another bauble, unworthy
of pursuit. It's joy we crave, not
meek, tepid, hula-hoopish happiness.
Of course that one hour of madness
and joy will cost—
derangement and sickness unto death.
Schumann's irony makes more sense
than any Euclidean axiom. But don't
tell anybody—they'll think you're crazy.

Disorder

The same equations that govern entropy
govern information theory.
Of course I don't get it, why should I?
But very interesting, strange bedfellows here.
Entropy, that demon of aging, decay and death
somehow bleats in the pulse of everyday data,
say, your receipt from Food Lion or the e-mail
you sent to Gloria or the grocery list taped
to your refrigerator.

           And we know too
that "information" relies upon noise and redundancy
which means that most of it belongs
with the garbage—and yet if it weren't for
that garbage it would glut our minds
and like Luria's mnemonist we could not function
given the avalanche of novelty we suffer
each sunrise.

           So what ho? Why does any of this
pertain and how should we proceed?
I guess we could say that we should not proceed
since any procession means marching backwards
to the usual fifes and bagpipes;
perhaps what-is and what-is-not pertinent
were once inseparable, our Eng's and Chang's
of holy matrimony

Etruscans

D.H. Lawrence found them heavy
into death, history-lost souls
with a language like no other
in Europe—they left behind scarce
literary or historical records.
They called themselves Rasenna
and DNA evidence links them
to Anatolia, now Turkey.
Myth has it that Romulus and Remus
who founded Rome were Etruscans
and they did indeed control the place
before the Romans themselves
assimilated them out of existence.
But why concern ourselves with still
another vanished people? Why fret
over the others as well—Hittites,
Sumerians, Ostrogoths, Celts
and so many more?

Because the loss of anyone at all
should freeze us in our tracks,
should remind us that there is more
lost than found, that memento mori
is our song played backwards,
that without them, however invisible,
however obscure, we who now strut
about the hemispheres like bantams,
would not sing at all, nor dance
nor wonder who they were and why
they departed and why we care
or don't care.

Raining Ants

We found hundreds of frozen ants
in my grandmother's refrigerator,
fat cadavers spilling like rice.
We blew them out with an electric fan,
swept the debris into a dustpan.
A few stuck to the freezer,
affixed, I guess, with some
tough death glue. They probably came
from an arid hill under the house
eager to raid the cache.

My grandmother was in the hospital
fighting another kind of freeze.
She wouldn't be back.
When I dumped the stiff corpses
into a garbage bag
they sounded like raindrops
battering a tarpaulin.
It's raining everywhere,
on the moon, on Mars,
on the roof, inside my head.

It rains in an old lady's refrigerator,
rains ants. When cold
sweeps down from the north
to this oven of a city,
there will be more ice
than we can chip away with picks.
Dead ants will rattle in our bodies
like furious teeth.

Fool Such as I

My wife and I escort the girls to their piano recital,
an otherwise vapid Wednesday afternoon,
and the only other person present is the piano teacher,
but it's nice and private, the way we like,
and Claire, now seventeen, has decided to quit piano
so this will be her last "concert," and Maddie,
fourteen, will continue with it though it saddens her
to think of lessons without her sister
since they have gone together for at least five years
(but Maddie holds it all it, the great overwhelming forces
that subvert us all, unlike Claire who erupts like Vesuvius) . . .

well, teacher hands us the programs and I prepare
my camera, and Cathy and I sit together in front
of the great Steinway holding hands as the girls begin
with a duet from Sousa, "Semper Fidelis,"
and I feel the wrenching begin, the sinking in my heart,
for I once played that song too on the flute
in junior high and my dad played it before us all
in the Air Force band, he on piccolo over in Karachi
while I was being born, so the piece has anchors
dragging it down to murky depths, for me anyway,
and my throat begins to constrict because
my girls look so intent and beautiful in their concert dresses,
so grown up, not the little monkeys they were yesterday,
and yesterday always means more than yesterday,
it means years ago, when they were three and seven,
plunking Chopsticks on piano keys,
and that time too passes before my eyes,
and then Maddie takes solo with a dolorous Bach prelude
which causes me soul such mayhem I can no longer hold back
and release a torrential, gasping sob . . .

oh I try to disguise it as a cough, or a laugh, something else,
but all eyes turn on me as Cathy grips my hand tighter
and Claire leans over to ask "Are you ok, Daddy?"
and that question precipitates still more sobs
because, no, I am not all right,
and I leave the room in the middle of Maddie's piece,
something I wouldn't miss for the entire universe
and all its bounty, but I must, for I have disrupted the recital,
and I'm sure the teacher doesn't know what to think,
but now the sobs gush forth as I stand outside an exit
and I know I must return soon, knowing also that more sobs
will ensue, that I have made a fool of myself again
and Cathy and the girls will rib me about it without mercy
for as long as I live . . .

so I return to my seat
and throw up my hands when the piano teacher
gazes my way and I mewl, "I'm sorry, I'm just
a sentimental old Italian, my dad used to play that song,"
which isn't true, the Bach anyway, but how can I, a grown man,
admit that the music's beauty, my daughter's adroit fingers,
the memories all gushing forth, how
can I explain that these are sobs of ransacked love,
that the past has caught up with me in this plain practice room
with its magnificent grand piano, that I have also
zoomed into the future where my girls are headed,
a future that I will miss, that maybe someday
I cannot take my seat as they play their finest concert
without me, without my camera, that I can't conceive
of just not being there for them, of not listening,
sobbing as they play, making a fool of myself
over and over and over again forever,
for my daughters . . .

and girls, if you ever read this,
forgive me, I'm sorry for interrupting your show,
it was not my show after all, not mine, not mine
and yet mine.

IV.

Morning Walk by the River

As I began my trek on the gravel path
toward the river I was met by an older woman
coming from the other direction.
As we approached each other she smiled,
said, "How we doing today?"

So I stopped to tell her that I was dismayed
by the prospect of the heat death of the universe
trillions of years in the future since it meant
that everything we know—nature, families,
children, the music of Beethoven and Mozart,
the complete works of Shakespeare, the sculptures
of Rodin and Michelangelo, the paintings of Van Gogh,
well, they all meant nothing, everything was doomed,
had no ultimate purpose, our existences caput,
the whole shebang, meaningless. I told her
that war, disease, famine, drought, politics, death—
they all annulled the momentary pleasures
of, say, eating a strawberry, of love and kissing,
of cupcakes, finding that pot of gold . . .
I would have expounded further, for I had lots
to say . . .

But she cut me off, looked me sadly in the eyes:
"Mister, the Doc gives me two months to live."
I stood appalled as she hobbled off
in the other direction. I stood aghast, wanted
to rush back and hug her, apologize for my
paltry concerns and intellectual apprehensions
though her words corroborated mine, though
they chilled me to the bone, though they
issued in the very dread heat death of the universe
I feared, a very very cold affair.

Sweet Sorrow

My girls left today for Hollins where they
are students. They brought Cinnamon
back to Roanoke with them.
You should have seen her cavorting in the leaves
of our back yard, her tail awag as I fed her
bacon-flavored treats.
And I, absorbed with finance and business,
waiting on the phone for endless menus,
only, when finally connected, to hear:
"I am either away from my desk or helping
another customer. At the sound of the beep,
please leave your name, and message."
I left nothing.

Now I lean back in the Subaru listening
to Mozart's Jupiter Symphony as I plan
my approach to the massive, industrial building
where I shall explain my case to someone
without ears.
Bittersweet to tell my daughters goodbye,
bittersweet to stroke Cinnamon goodbye.
And why? When not purely sweet?

I told Claire that "happiness"
is superficial, a Frisbee distraction;
we're after privileged, fleeting joys—
always free, easy, simple and unexpected.
Catching sight of daffodils fluttering
and dancing in the breeze, sniffing lacquer
on a banister that transports us back to an ocean
of accumulated honeyed teardrops annulling
for a while the military-industrial complex
of capital and dreary sad waste time.

There's Cinnamon romping in the back yard
of my mind, the girls waving goodbye,
the rare, ordinary, angelic split seconds
of our days!

Porn Stars

They have achieved the Freudian zion
of polymorphous perversity beyond the crib,
evolved into pure genital, young mostly,
supple, tattooed and be-ringed to the point
of disfigurement, though some, pruned with age,
hormonal Abe's and Sarah's, venerable,
vericosed laughing stocks, hungry for a last twitch . . .

     . . . as I think of Gross National Product, the Dow,
lawyers in vulture suits, foundations, think tanks,
R&D, actuarial tables, ashen Swiss bankers,
I turn to these innocents with relief and admiration,
they, willing to risk everything, name, future,
disease, their lives, for ecstasy;
they defy rendezvous with manifest destiny,
would jack off the president; they, untouchables
who live for touch, who stroke, probe, knead, lick
the flesh of the Other as strobes blast,
cameras whir; they drown in a glandular soup,
die for joy and a little cash to get by.

And later, the seedy biographies of some
who achieved a speck of notoriety,
overdosed, suicidal, abused, found battered
and comatose in an alley . . . the moral,
obviously, pious and solemn: *the wages of sin.*
And yet their faces gleam in celluloid
as the juices flow and they begin the ascent
to a rapturous apex . . .

the drowsy, oceanic smiles,
parted lips, gasp and release, the letting go,
the only heaven on earth, slimy with fluids,
disgusting, aroused, the unbeautiful repose
of those who live for nothing else,
who can't resist, who will die
in lonely motel rooms beyond the talons
of that sublime, sublimated civilization
we erect despite, without and because of them.

Mayday, or, Prayer to Bob Villa

Mushrooms now sprout on the lawn
and, of course, we fear black mold and radon.
The roof leaks and one of the foundation supports
has crumbled. Oh, the cracks in that old plaster
make us so uneasy we drink potent wine every night.
I want to call Bob Vila and beg him to move in,
take care of us. When we're gone, Bob,
you can have the house and all our possessions,
just keep us afloat, hack down those mushrooms,
patch those leaks, suck out that radon from deep
within the bowels of the planet, pipe it elsewhere,
to Nebraska maybe or some pristine state.

We're not up to it, Bob, we joint debtors
in this fiscal and survival enterprise.
I've heard they can compress the ashes of those
who choose cremation into pure blue diamonds.
Think of it. We'll donate ourselves as well.
You'll be a rich man, Bob. Just save us.
I believe I've begun the transformation already—
look at these fuzzy blue veins streaking like straw
from my heart. There's a section in the IRS
manual called "Death of the Taxpayer,"
and I've circled the important items
to facilitate our transaction. Bob, I'm not asking
anymore, I'm demanding. You know tools,
how to make things level, square joints—
we, we joint debtors, can't even choose
        the right shade of latex.

Please, we need you, we worship you,
take it all, whatever your pleasure . . . just
keep us breathing long as you can.

Stuffed Artichokes

It's Easter, so naturally there will be food.
I call my mother long distance and after
the Happy Easter's she will tell me what
she's fixed for the family down there.
The usual turkey, a spinach casserole
with grillards, French green beans, and
ah, the stuffed artichokes. I hear the words
and know I must try to create what only
she can, since she cooks by instinct,
by religion, and I, so far along already,
just beginning to learn. I ask
for the recipe, knowing I will have
to decipher into more precise terms,
those of an auditor or accountant,
more schematic, without the magic, if
I am to reproduce the artichokes
with even a smidgen of their glory.
Well, she laughs, that's an easy one,
and repeats the old story about the secret
handed down from a great-grandmother
in Genoa who sold ravioli in the streets.

First, she says, chop up a bulb of garlic
and a pile of flat leaf parsley . . .
a whole bulb, that's a lot of garlic,
I'm thinking . . . and add about half
a container of grated Romano and parmesan,
oh, and about the same amount of bread
crumbs, the Italian kind from Progresso.
Just put them in a pan with about an inch
of water and douse the tops with olive oil—
don't forget to cut off the stems and points
at the top. That's it, let them steam.

How long? I ask. Until you can pick off
the leaves real easily. Do it on a low
to medium flame. That's a lot of garlic,
I can't help saying, rough on the stomach.
She laughs, it's for eight people, what
you thought it was just one artichoke?

I'll have to try it, I tell her, knowing
I will never try it, that at some step
in the process I will burn the leaves,
add the wrong number of breadcrumbs,
go slightly higher on one cheese or the other,
use the wrong olive oil. I hope you do,
she says, pleased, mother happy.
But remember, the recipe is a secret.
Don't tell anybody.

Words

Tell them I've lived a wonderful life.
—allegedly Wittgenstein's
last words on this deathbed

I hate the word colleague, but what the hell,
this colleague of mine—an ally, not enemy—,
tells me the other day he's been diagnosed
with prostate cancer. He's my age, maybe younger,
so I'm all ears as usual when the scythe swings.
And I feel the anchor of woe for both of us
begin its descent into my gut. Jesus, I say.
But he's perky and cheerful enough, explains
how next week he'll undergo some new procedure
that doesn't require chemo. The oncologist—
another dread word —assures him that 75 percent
of those treated retain normal bladder control.
And a lesser percentage can still get hard-ons
(he uses the phrase penile function)
with the aid of Viagra. Jesus, Jesus, I don't say,
suppose . . .

They don't think it's spread, he says, we'll find out
on Tuesday. Tuesday, I think, is a word.
So is cancer. Death, suffering, mutilation, all words.
I once learned in a linguistics class that they
precede facts, create reality—though by now
it's clear we're dealing with supreme caca.

What are the symptoms? I ask uneasily.
None! he declares as if elated by the irony.
Caught it during a routine checkup. So, he warns,
be sure to let them stick their fingers up your ass
every year. Hey, he digs his eyes into mine,

I don't wanna die.
Jesus is a word. Die. Die. I don't wanna.
Fingers up the ass. Lopping off a ball or two.
Wearing Kotex, like a woman.

I don't go to doctors, I say, gave up on it.
The horror is too stately.
It's their job to find something. Maybe if they
don't, it will go away, maybe, maybe, maybe . . .
I must have disturbed my colleague.
His face paled, he edged away backwards,
clipped an abrupt "see ya,"and fled.
Pain clutched my groin with fat gorilla fingers.
But no symptoms, he said, no symptoms.
Only insidious words.

Snow

oh, it's beautiful all right,
glorious even, peachy, nature
at its most regal, yep, all that . . .
until your boot sinks into it

like that woman you knew
years ago, beautiful, stunning,
enough trouble
to frostbite your entire past

Just a Note

Babe, when you sent me
that wishbone in the mail
I snapped it in half
and got the short end.

So I'm returning
the other side, the good side,
to you via media mail.
There's still a little
meat on it.

Secret

I like poems I understand
which doesn't mean
I don't like poems
I don't understand

has less to do with clarity
or obscurity

than hearing
the key click
and knowing you've
unlocked the door

or kissing someone
you love
when it feels
like you're kissing
yourself

Rife with Passage

We savor continuity in our lives
despite dips and surges slithering
like sine waves through space,
orobus with tail in mouth.

We want the light switch always
where it is, the toothpaste snug
in its tube, our keys cuddled
in their nook . . .

but every now and then
some cataclysmic rupture
may render us instantly
rigor mortised corpses,
the viper curling through
ragged eye sockets,

or,

may Hawaiify us into
sensuous nuns gliding through
pristine colonnades,
no, not nuns, ourselves
exponentialized, abluted,
forgiven, shriven, purified
out of ourselves. . .
an orgasmic twitch of the eye.

Snapshot of Pablo Neruda

I stare at the photo of Pablo Neruda
on the dust jacket of his *Collected Poems*.
The name, of course, Pablo Neruda
is what makes me stare.

Without the name it could well
be that photo of my great uncle
Achille who played a very bad cello.
Or perhaps anyone's crusty uncle,
the one who never comes
to your parties, the one who
kicked his wife into the street.

Replace it with the photo of someone else
and I'd still stare. Pablo Neruda
could look like anyone in Houston or Madrid
or Olympus.

All in a Night's Work

We're at the Skyvue Drive-In, front row,
so close we need to drip our heads flat on the back of the seat
to see the screen. It's ok because the roof of the car
has become transparent and we gaze through it.
There's no movie, just a flickering backdrop buzzing
with frenzied dragonflies.
Next to us, to the left, a cute red Sunbeam
from England bulges with protoplasmic gobs
each containing several distinct personalities.
One wears old horn-rimmed glasses that swirl in the gel.
We don't know what lies to the right. The right no longer exists.
Nor can we remember how many packed into our car.
Now it's just Mom sitting behind the steering wheel,
my sister next, then me, shotgun.
I fiddle with a clunky metal loudspeaker and try to light
a green mosquito repellant coil at the same time.
The speaker wire is so taut
I can barely hook the baffle clip onto the window.

We don't care much that there's no movie
especially since out friend Jim raps on my window
to ask if we want to throw some shot-puts.
I'm null on the idea but Ruthie really wants to
so I tag along—and I guess we leave Mom at this point
because we never see her again. I shuffle on the grass
while Jim and Ruthie hurl the shot-puts far as they can,
which isn't impressive. But here I lose my sister as well
and wander into a dense, clinging fog. It's greenish and sticky,
I feel pretty lousy and need to get somewhere.
Then Will shows up—
he's my brother-in-law decades later—a guy from Scotland
who can imitate Elvis on his bag-pipes.
He's crying so I drift over to see what's wrong.
"I don't want this dream to end," he howls.

"What dream?" I ask . . . which opens up a can of not worms
but philosophic hors d'oeuvres on death. He says
it won't be so bad because look at sleep, we have
such beautiful dreams. Hamlet's perchance, I mumble,
though I don't like this turn.

Started out at a movie, now I remember, with Tony Curtis
and Kirk Douglas, *The Vikings,* where Tony and Kirk
are lovers . . . wait, that's *Spartacus:* "I love you, Spartacus."
They're the same movie. Everything is the same movie.
The guys wear little skirts, or kilts, maybe pantaloons.
It's so hard to straighten your facts these days.
Will and I linger in the mist discussing death
while, I guess, Mom has driven home, and Ruthie
and Jim go to Melba Ice Cream for banana splits.
Reality begins to taper here, constricts itself
like the tip of one of those light cones in physics:
all the options but one—the one you're in—
evaporate. I even sit up in bed and feel around
to make sure I am where I am.

Slowly I focus on the wallpaper, the furniture,
my robe hanging from a hall tree.
Somebody outside yells, "Fuckkkkk."
The clock reads five a.m. No choice but to hobble
down the stairs and spoon a little coffee yogurt
out of its tub. Something's wrong with the fridge—
it squawks like wild geese.
A slug bulges on one of the designer tiles.
I inform Will that I'm going home
and advise him to get some sleep.
Ruthie, you shouldn't hang out with Jim,
remember what happened to him in law school?
Mom, you're too old now to work. I don't approve.

This yogurt tastes so good I want to take it slow,
plop down on the sofa and switch on a movie.
Bright scintillant screen at first,
then this ancient flick . . . can it be?
The Vikings or *Spartacus*. There's Tony kissing Kirk
on the lips, some tongue action as well.

Go back to Ruth, Will; don't brood on death.
What's the point?
It's the species that counts, not any one of us,
we're all conjoined in a kind of spiritual jelly.
Something bites my forehead. When I swat
my glasses fly across the room. I'm so blind
I've got to feel around to find the damned things . . .
and realize they're not mine. Somebody else
lost his glasses in my living room at five a.m.
I finish off the yogurt. Back up the stairs.
Slide under the covers.
On my back, knowing I'll never get back to sleep.
Do I only imagine the dragonfly—down here
we call them mosquito hawks—
darting at my forehead like a missile with wings?
Pale, fuzzy light already seeps into the room.
This night is over.

By noon life should get pretty boring, sort of like
sewing buttons onto your sleeve or filing papers
into pigeonholes.
But that's what pays—mending, sorting, enterprise,
efficiency and sunlight—
not this other fantastic crap we don't even remember
once it flares sweetly, sacredly, out of nowhere.

Kindergarten Poem

Each day, parked in front of the school
waiting for my daughter, I see the same man
pushing a wheelchair up the steep hill
that leads to just about where I slouch
in the bucket seat listening to Schubert.
It's a struggle, he's not young,
either father or grandfather
of the child he pushes, a boy who wears
thick glasses and has feathery white hair.
His head droops forward, sometimes rolls
to one side or the other. The man always stops
to straighten it, then pats him on the shoulder.

You can tell it's love, more than love,
this extra devotion, this most bitter ministering.
I don't know what they're doing out here;
the child is a first grader from what I hear
and class is in session. Could be the man,
let's call him father, wants to take
his stricken boy out for air
or just extricate him for a while
from the madness of walls and desks.
He is punctual and steady, prepared,
equipped with Kleenex, inhalers, prescriptions.
I admire him enormously but must refuse
to think about him, or the boy.
Word is, it's terminal.

I wait for my robustly healthy daughter
to spring from the building, rush down the steps
and toss me her backpack. It's her sassy smile
that I need to expect, to remember each day.
The boy in the wheelchair never smiles.
He seems mostly asleep in some dream world

all his own; nor does the father smile,
though he feasts on every fraction of a second
with the child. How he endures day after day,
the poise of absolute defeat somehow defeating itself—
as if to convey a kind of joy I hope I'll never know.
But I can't dwell on it. I'm waiting for my daughter.
The bell has rung. She will come barging out the door
any minute now. We parents congregate near
the concrete steps and I imagine, in some sense,
hold our breaths. When the children flutter forth
in happy commotion there's always a twinge
of panic if we don't see our own right away.

The man pushes his boy on the sidewalk
amid all of us. We nod, he nods, and then we clutch
our children's frail hands and lead them away
to cars and head for home. Today my daughter
says she's had a bad day. She's about to cry.
Her toy watch fell off and some boy's shoe
crushed it into a pile of plastic splinters.
I assure her I will buy another.
Can't mess with time, I laugh,
and wait for the giggle,
though I don't think she gets the joke.

We drive home singing the new song she's learned

button you must wander, wander, wander—

The sun blasts through our windows like sweet cream.
She's buckled tightly in her car seat
and I rivet an eye into the rear view
to make sure she doesn't disappear.
I feel an ease akin to that of trees lining the road,

their red, yellow and purple leaves
ready to unhinge . . .
Suddenly at the stop sign
I want to scream . . . but I don't.

V. Advent

Dec 1:

All shall be well, and all shall be well, and all manner of thing shall be well.
—Julian of Norwich

I too have sought for most of my life. I seek now. Where is the
rebirth? In what stable, what alley, what cul de sac? Anchorite,
saint, have we not all survived a Black Death at some point or
another? It induced visions for you, though often my eyesight fails,
and I espy only a vessel or two on the horizon. Or my own blood
vessels of vitreous humor or pathos. when shall all be well? In
whose heart? Today as dawn bloomed gloriously on the horizon, I
stood on the porch awaiting a milkman who never came. You went
blind with sickness for a spell. How emerge from the shadows with
a swath of revelations? Tell me how.

Dec 2:

What has been is what will be, and what has been done is what will be done, and there is nothing new under the sun.
— Ecclesiastes

What you fear most is what will happen.
— Caesar Pavese

Nietzsche's eternal return or the yo-yo cycles of the universe: Bang then Crunch then Bang, Crunch, *ad infinitum*. Our brains cannot tolerate infinity, nor Aristotle a vacuum. What is infinity? Why, some say it amounts to zero. Vacuum! Imagine. Being and nothingness, bride and groom married by shotgun. I've had it with fear, sent it packing on the way to Ultima Thule. Tis the season to be jolly. Ho ho ho. Get me some rum cake, rock by the Buck stove fire and dream about hummingbirds. And wouldn't you know— our little dog, Cinnamon, comes round and begs for a crumb. Dog spelled backwards is God.

Dec 3:

. . . and is to be at an instant suddenly
—Isaiah

Like everything, right? Once you say NOW, it's the past. The past
is your mind and mine, the future too diffuse to call until it too at
an instant sudden becomes the past. The postman delivered the
gold, frankincense and myrrh to the wrong house. Let me consult
with the Wise Men—Melchior, Caspar and Balthazar, magi, or
eenie-meenie-mo. William James: "Wisdom is knowing what to
overlook." I don't want to overlook the slightest smidgen, the
cracked black walnut husk on our deck, the praying mantis glued
to our storm door window, the bells of St. Rosa de Lima on Bayou
Road. Omnia pertains, miss the crocus, miss the universe. I want
off this ferry. I want to walk on water with that man. Lazarus, him
hip to it all, came back in a spiffy tux and bow tie. I have ordered
some spats from L. L. Bean, Inc. Delivery takes time, no instant
sudden, unless I read it all wrong.

Dec 4:

. . . your adversary the devil, as a roaring lion, walketh about, seeking whom he may devour . . .

—1 Peter 5:8

I met him back then at Las Casas de los Marinos on Decatur Street, the scent of hops from the Jax Beer Brewery suffusing the place, "You are My Sunshine" blasting out from the steamboat calliope on the river. Dapper little creep. "Get thee behind me," I cried, and, poof! he vanished. I'll never forget the tears in his eyes. Want to exorcise all demons, jujus, sirens, ghouls and phantoms for the festive season. Want some King Cake and egg nog. Want absolution and a sackcloth and ashes rubbed into the forehead. Want nothing and everything, the only avenue to peace of mind. Love them Buddhist koans. They make you stop and think, though better not to think, just breath long as you can. Deeply.

Dec 5:

What is my strength, that I should wait? And what is my end, that I should be patient?

—Book of Job, 6-11

And birth begat calling and calling begat betrayal and betrayal begat crucifixion and crucifixion begat resurrection . . . wow, lots of begatting. Jesus been gone a long time. I'm waiting in line at Walmart, one cashier in the entire store. This is what it's come to. I'm waiting in line at the DMV, at the Post Office, at the counter of Cosmo's Diner, at the gas pumps, at the ER where my daughter squirms in pain, at Starbucks, at . . . at everywhere. Waiting. What percentage of our lives? Waiting for Logos, for the witch doctor, for absolution, for the check to arrive, the supper for which we sing, revelation, for the dream to end. Patience is a disease. Waiting. Look, a break in the line, rush for it, it's a stampede, watch your back! No at-an-instant-suddenly these days. Whither green pastures and the Rose of Sharon? At an instant bit by bit.

Dec 6:

. . . Take it and eat it up; and it shall make thy belly bitter, but it shall be in thy mouth sweet as honey. And I took the little book out of the angel's hand and ate it up; and it was in my mouth sweet as honey: and as soon as I had eaten it, my belly was bitter.

—Book of Revelations

"Nothing sweet as you-ooh a-as honey comes from bees"— remember that song? Of course you don't, way before your time. A lousy song anyway but sticks in the mind like some dismal ingot. And thus I refused to take and eat and thereby avoided both the sweet and the sour. Regrets ever since. Come back with the offering! Come back, angel of paradox, return that little book to the library. The fines get stiffer every sudden instant. Bitter herbs doused with sugar. *That which I should have done, I did not do.*

Dec 7:

But I'm already inside Dolly's Pastry Shack on Monkey Hill and refuse to leave, ah, she of lambent eye and fiery hair, she sleek and Aphroditean, my cosmic wife of the shamans, she, my other salvation, she, the apple fritter of mine eye. Keep away, never. She rubs me down, wipes the ashes from my forehead, stitches up the sackcloth, ministers unto me—succor, balm, peace of mind and flesh. The Lord giveth, the Lord taketh away. Why give then take?—give and take. Some miserable game of retribution? I love thee, Ariadne. All your scripture, not worth a single strand of Dolly's hair. My darling, my darling, my life and my bride. Blueberries with cream like in *Elvira Madigan.*

Dec 8:

Go to the ant, thou sluggard; consider her ways, and be wise
                                   —Proverbs 6:6-8

Madam I'm Adam. Who wants to scurry about day in, day out, by the sweat of their brow? I don't blame you for the apple. You got a bad rap. I dared you but was too craven to admit it until now. You were feisty and flamboyant and not one to cringe. And I ate it too—knowledge, good and evil, poisoned. Toil, disease, death . . . ever since. We were children before the fig leaves, the shame, the expulsion. That garden was childhood, the Fall, coming of age, puberty, hormones. Certainly not your fault despite those who *j'accuse* you to this day. And yet I do wonder about the Architect's faulty design, the slaying of us all, in tandem, relentlessly. Mostly, though, I miss the rib. Hi ho hi ho, it's off to work we go, again, the livelong day, some nights too. No overtime either, no pension.

Dec 9:

You too? Papa, he has them every night. That hand, that
handwriting on the wall (mene, mene, tekel)—Nebuchadnezzar's
ill omen. No Daniel around to interpret mine—the Subaru coasting
along a steep mountain road, a steep drop off the crag, a mud slide,
the brakes burn out, driving blind. Though obviously some sort of
out-of-control anxiety scenario. And who is not out of control? The
universe is out of control. Zorba the Greek: "Life *is* trouble, so
buckle up your belt." Recurrent, though, as if the path too narrow,
the mud too thick, the vehicle defective, the crag—the drop, the
giving up, the end of the road. Rolling Stones: "Then I awoke/Was
this some kind of joke/Much to my surprise/I opened
up my eyes." In another land, all right, where I held your hand in
mine and all was well and shall be well. Which the dream?

Dec 10:

You hurled me into the deep, into the very heart of the seas, and the currents swirled about me; all your waves and breakers swept over me.
—Book of Jonah 2:30

Then the whale, three days and three nights, a sort of shamanic, hole-in-the-ground, enterprise. What did I discern inside aside from wet, glistening organs? I was pissed off at God, you see, for not punishing the malefactors of Nineveh. What mercy allows evil to thrive while innocents are crushed? Hey, I've read my Blake, I know the deal with tigers and lambs. Doesn't quite convince me And, hey again, don't think I didn't enjoy spending time inside Monstro. Like a return to the womb, happy oblivion, secure, content, satiated. Close to Thanatos, sure, but so what? Hi, Mom, I love you.

—your little Oedipus

Dec 11:

Lift up your eyes and look from the place where you are
                                        —Genesis 13:4

*Where you come from is gone, where you thought you were going to never
was there, and where you are is no good unless you can get away from it.*
                                        —Flannery O'Connor, *Wise Blood*

Been saying that my whole damn life. Anyplace better than where
you at, like this dive, the Seven Seas Bar, in the Quarter, full of
drunks & punks & brutes smashing ouzo bottles on each other's
skulls. How'd I wind up here, I raised genteel, uptown, I who once
played flute in the philharmonic? Even my language has
deteriorated. So I lifted my eyes, as advised by none other, and
what do I see? A thick mire, like my friend Gimpel saw, only this
one thicker, because I ain't no fool. It's beginning to look a
smidgen like Christmas though. They're strung twinkling, colorful
lights outside the door. Some freak inserted one tip of the wire into
his mouth for a rush and got electrocuted. See what I mean?
Maybe Santa is just baby Jesus returned as an old coot tying to
rectify.

Dec 12:

Can't be, can't be, can't be. Hitler, Stalin, Pol Pot, Vlad the Impaler, Elagabalus, Genghis Khan, Torquemada, Al Capone, Charles Manson, Iago, Claggart, the Misfit, the image of God? Maybe a few—the Dalai Lama, Jesus the man, St. Francis, a few, maybe. Which chart outweighs? Better to say we created God in our own image. That would account for all the atrocities, massacres, wars, murders, rapes, pillaging, the Spanish Inquisition, the crucifixions. Are the ways of God mysterious to man or are the ways of man mysterious to God? How could that be, though, given omniscience? Omniscience seems inadequate.

Dec 13:

This is the first and principal benefit caused by this arid and dark night of contemplation: the knowledge of oneself and of one's misery.
        —San Juan de la Cruz, *Dark Night of the Soul*

I don't know, Maw, can't seem to get into the right mood yet, you know, like Bing dreaming of a White Christmas or that song, "Joy to the World." I'm working on it, don't think I'm not. I'm trying the advice of Mr. James: *Want to be cheerful? Act cheerfully.* Could amount to some supreme behavioristic caca, though. Don't worry, be happy. What button do I press? Lots of people in the same ark throughout history I'm told. Brain chemistry, skimpy serotonin. They ought to add it to Coca-Cola. Then there's that German, Vaihinger, with his *as if* philosophy: Feel down? Act *as if* you're up; Dead? act *as if* you're still alive! Isn't that lying to yourself? "Here's the Season to be Jolly," though difficult to attain when one watches the news every night. But I'm working on it, Hi Ho . . . look! A hummingbird flitting above our purple cone flowers! There, you see, a moment of privilege, small good thing, bestowal, gift, wondrous hummingbird. I need to pet Cinnamon real fast. Got her some nice doggie treats—bacon, chicken & beef.

Dec 14:

Circumcise therefore the foreskin of your hearts, therefore and do not be stiff necked any longer.

—Deuteronomy 10:16

Yikes, sounds painful. The ancient remedy for excess cholesterol and triglycerides, maybe the cartilage stiffening of arthritis? Whatever. Physician, heal thyself! They took the knife to me when I was born, way back, and no more circumcision of anything. Heart? Neck? Feels good to rotate and crack it, wouldn't trade for anything except a younger neck. And neck is a kind of phallic symbol, right? Longer than wide unless you're goiter unfortunate. All I want for Christmas is my younger self, a looser neck, a beating heart *sans* built-in obsolescence and the great gift to believe in Santa, the elves, Mr. Bingle, Rudolph, all that schlock. Oh, and the manger, the star, Mary Mother of us All, that whole dream. And whatever I get.

Dec 15:

Your cheeks are beautiful with earrings, your neck with strings of jewels
—Song of Solomon 1:10

But not piercings of any kind, nose rings or those grotesque holes
punched in the earlobes. Maybe a tiny discreet tattoo of a peacock
on the small of your back, the most underrated part of a woman's
body. But not you, babe. You're perfect wearing only flesh
unblemished by metal or jewels. Your eyes, the sapphires, your
lips the rubies, your tongue the pendant. Just as you are, Eve
(though I prefer to call you Cookie, since you're delicious). How
we feasted upon each other on Annunciation Street after that spider
bit you at the Absolute Café and I massaged Benadryl into your
welts. Or when you forgot who you were in Alabama and insisted
you had to leave the motel to meet up with you lunatic relatives at
the local asylum. I pinned you down and you never looked more
ravishing. Or that cheap AWOL joint in Destin with mirrors on the
ceiling and every wall. Oh, how we made up for post-lapsarian
desolation. I, Solomon, otherwise solemn, declare rapturously,
made wise, not blinded, by love.

Dec 16:

Things looking up, honey. The darkness had surrounded us though we didn't go out and buy a goddam new car. But we did drive and looked out where we were going. Not the path of Childe Roland this time, a serene meadow instead, bluebirds, sheep mesmerized by the shepherd's bucolic pipes. And the little timber cabin Papa built back during the Time of Pleasure, a sedate plume of smoke rising from its chimney, communing with the clouds. There we disported ourselves, comported, disported again. And shall again. And when we do, it's Christmas and the New Year and Easter all at once, *la petite mort* and resurrection conjoined. Ah, love, we're back in the garden for a spell, spent, charged, transfigured. I supped honey from the comb; you, nectar from the stalk. Holy days.

Dec 17:

All the winged insects that walk on all fours are detestable to you.
                                                    —Leviticus 11:20

The lovely butterfly, ladybug, the sweet honeybee, detestable? Got
to watch the petty martinets; they yearn to tabulate your every
breath, like this Levi, dude, rules, rules, rules, anti-LGBQT, but
it's ok to own slaves from foreign countries; and be sure not to
make the beast with two backs with another man's female slave.
No adultery, please, and purify the burnt offerings, especially the
kidneys and liver. What soap should we use? So many choices in
Harris Teeter, it's paralyzing. Choose for me, drill sergeant. Never
mind, I'm going to visit the display in Audubon Park with Cookie.
Last time, one lighted atop her burning copper hair. What beauty
there, that bountiful epiphany.
Anti-Leviticus 1:1
ladybug on the lamp shade fringe

My first thought when I espied her clinging
To a decorative strand of the deco shade
Was revulsion, my first instinct to pinch
Her between my fingers and fling her
Into the box elder outside—
No insects in the house, disgusting.
But, as I prepared the assault, I noticed
How beautiful she was and how adamantly
She clung to that thread as if some ladybug
Lifeline for survival in this unnatural place.
An alien guest in my house from another kingdom!
So I turned off the lamp to avoid exposing her
To excess heat and bid her stay put
For as long as she so desired.

The next day she remained fixed in place
As if glued there, and I did nudge her off
Into my palm. She could not survive
In the house. I did not have to fling her
Into the bush; she spread her tiny wings
And flew toward the center, overjoyed
May you prosper, guest, and remember
The lampshade that attracted you.

Dec 18:

So they kept this matter to themselves, discussing what it meant to rise from the dead.

—Mark 9:10

I'll tell you what "rising from the dead' means. It means rising from the dead. No secret, no need for committees, colloquies, debate. Death and transfiguration, resurrection. What's to discuss? Almost as if they didn't quite believe it and had to figure out some PR to sell the idea. Check out Lazarus the leper. He came back, not much said about the second life though. Either you're dead or alive, or maybe both like Schrodinger's cat before somebody opens the lid. I've seen a few corpses in my time and they didn't look very happy. But let's go with Pascal—fifty, fifty, one fifty, MWF, the other, TThSat. Sunday up for grabs. Fierce hope tomorrow and tomorrow and tomorrow.

Dec 19:

My father used to say that nostalgia was a disease. If so, count me sick, for I am sore afflicted. I am writing a book entitled *The History of Memory,* a projected ten thousand volumes in fine print to be shelved in the Library of Alexandria. When our X-Terra broke down and had to be traded in, my youngest and final daughter, Madeleine, shed a tear and drew a carton of us sitting in the SUV waiting for the school bell to ring. I drove her to school every morning, always got there early so we had time to fiddle around and tell stories and jokes, maybe sing some goofy songs. Now, much later in the fugit of tempus, I gaze at the cartoon affixed to one side of the filing cabinet in my office. Next to it, the Victorian chromolithograph of a bouquet of flowers with the caption *Forget me Not.* And I remember hard those days of her childhood; such remembrance, embodied tears. The true sin is forgetting. Thou shalt not forget.

Dec 20:

Why sell doves, a kind of gourmet meal for the Pharisees? Just go slingshot some mangey pigeon in the Place d'Armes and fling them into the gumbo. But doves, beautiful doves? What manner of barbarian. Damn, like selling the Paraclete (on the wings of a dove), one-third of the celestial triumvirate, splinters of the cross at the corporate Flea Market. Why not sell you own Papa, and Mama too, while you're at it. Or yourself—though who would want to buy *you?* Bayou, LOL. Liquid cash for blood, silver for brain, Judas money. Blessed be the poor long as you ain't one of them. Root of all evil. Not merely root—stem, flower, the full catastrophe. Our presence in the vast, obscene emporium of presents—smart phones for the kids, a cookbook for Mama, a new catheter for Grandpa—the oligarchs stuffing our Georges into their eyes.

Dec 21:

Like that scene in *Zorba the Greek* when the human vultures
swooped into the bedroom of the dying woman, Zorba's beloved,
and razed the place in search of what they could steal—and they
would steal anything, a used handkerchief, a burnt-out light bulb, a
handleless screwdriver. Theft for the thrill of it. Bravo to Zorba for
sweeping them away, the old women in black veils and shawls, the
harpies. Like what happened to that old man on Elysian Fields
when he croaked—the grabbers showing up in mass to gather unto
themselves. Usurers, usurpers, the thieves, the aggrandizers. Good
Will and Salvation Army—where we donated Papa's closet full of
clothes for the poor. Christmas, no longer Christ's mass but the
Day of Greed, squatting among a heap of presents, tearing off the
wrapping paper . . . Cosmic Christ no longer pertinent, only the
acquisition of more, more, more & more. When do the meek
inherit the Earth? Mark your calendar for the advent.

Dec 22:

For what glory is it, if, when ye be buffeted for your faults, ye shall take it patiently? but if, when ye do well, and suffer for it, ye take it patiently. . .
—1 Peter 2:20

Or as the Buddhists put it: *make haste slowly.* The suffering, that's the thing. Who goes unscathed? To be cheerful, act cheerfully? All flesh is grass and witherith in the field—same dude speaking. The TV evangelist hops onto the stage in Elvis rhinestone and bangles, the crowds roar, spot Pentecostal wings of fire sashaying above their heads. He's worth ten million, drives a refurbished Rolls, has a dozen concubines who chew up the pages of the holy book as they minister unto him. Or Simeon Stylites, up on that pillar, exposed to the elements, fasting, praying, his disciples roping up the bucket back and forth on a pulley. The shaman buried alive for three days crying for a vision. Jesus in the desert. Everything is relative except what's relative, which is absolute. I am dumb to discern the parameters and exigencies—and therefore the injustice. Is the universe friendly, asked Einstein. Just look around. The evil malefactor lives exactly one century and little Dickie down the street, eight years old, lies in an iron lung. Padre Pio, make my palms bleed as well. That I could understand.

Dec 23:

And the Word became flesh and dwelt among us. . .
—Book of John I:14

The Word took me by surprise, seized me in darkness with neon talons, pushed me up the stairs into a different light, opaque, nimbused, aromatic. The Word smelled like cloudy fists of sweet olive smacking me silly and giddy. The Word was an angel of beatitude. The Word wasn't a word, corporealized elsewhere perhaps but not in this sanctuary. I wanted the pure Word, undistilled, the name-in-itself, the *sine qua non;* I wanted to clutch the quarks of the Word, before quarks, the quarks of quarks. When the Bodhisattva showed up with fried oyster po-boys and Barq's root beers, we sat on a patio of Annunciation Street and feasted. "Such," he smiles radiantly, "is the more-than-Word." I rushed home to announce to Cookie that I had been enlightened but she too laughed and laughed and laughed. "You have horse radish dripping down your chin," she laughed. That was the point though. I had devoured the Word with relish, sublime in the pedestrian. God in everything, even the motes of our dust.

Dec 24:

Not, after all, a pretty or fit remembrance for Christmas Eve, eh?
Nor Leda and the Swan, though who can ignore the parallels:
Mary/Paraclete? Cosmic in the mundane-quotidian, sublime in the
pedestrian—mystic magic. Choose to believe? If it makes you feel
better, why not? If it gets you up in the morning, why not? If it
soothes your mind, why not? As for Susanna, I remember her, and
yes, beauteous to behold. Should we not notice and rather smolder
inside? One of the apostles (I forget which) reminds us that lust in
the heart is tantamount to the deed itself. I reject the logic. When I
first beheld my Cookie, I surged with desire. Not solely physical,
though much of that too. But her mind, her essence, her kindness
and succor, her everything. What is lust? Do you not lust for your
beloved as did holy Solomon? Or is it a matter of *what's in a
name?* The Word made flesh or the Flesh made word. It's what
Jimmy Carter admitted to in a *Playboy* interview once. The human
condition, our need for connection and fructification. Punish the
despoilers, the violators, those who boast about grabbing women
by their genitalia. Jimmy's out building houses for the poor at
ninety years old. Spare the smitten heart. Understand. Separate the
wheat from the chaff. Chaff to the hogs. Pity Onan.

Dec 25:

Mommy, Daddy, he came, he came! And drank the cup of coffee you left on the kitchen table! He came, he came . . . as they unwrap their presents from under the tree, presents we spent the night before wrapping and sliding under the tree. Watching children smile with delight, what greater transport? And someone else may also have come. So here we gather again in the fullness of time, together, a reprieve of sorts, the scent of turkey and holly and cranberries, the old and the young, the lighted candles, the carols. I in my kerchief, Ma in her cap—or is it the other way around? And what to my wondrous eyes . . .? Though that was last night. Today is not yet tonight.

Let us on this day, at least, set aside all apprehension and misapprehension, all doubt, all regrets and acedia of soul. Let the lamp affix its beam on shadows and evaporate them. At least for this day. Let's carpe diem the hours before and after the feast. Let's give thanks if only to each other. May we even pray together. And make haste slowly. Look, a V of geese honking over the rooftops! A praying mantis on the doorknob! Them lilies of the field! Happy birthday, Son of Man.

About the Author

Four volumes of Louis Gallo's poetry, *Archaeology, Scherzo Furiant, Crash and Clearing the Attic,* are now available. *Why is there Something Rather than Nothing?* and *Leeway & Advent* will be published in the near future. His work appears in *Best Short Fiction 2020.* A novella, "The Art Deco Lung," will soon be published in *Storylandia.* National Public Radio aired a reading and discussion of his poetry on its "With Good Reason" series (December 2020). His work has appeared or will shortly appear in *Wide Awake in the Pelican State* (LSU anthology), *Southern Literary Review, Fiction Fix, Glimmer Train, Hollins Critic, Rattle, Southern Quarterly, Litro, New Orleans Review, Xavier Review, Glass: A Journal of Poetry, Missouri Review, Mississippi Review, Texas Review, Baltimore Review, Pennsylvania Literary Journal, The Ledge, storySouth, Houston Literary Review, Tampa Review, Raving Dove, The Journal (Ohio), Greensboro Review* and many others. Chapbooks include *The Truth Changes, The Abomination of Fascination, Status Updates,* and *The Ten Most Important Questions.* He is the founding editor of the now defunct journals, *The Barataria Review* and *Books: A New Orleans Review.* His work has been nominated for the Pushcart Prize several times. He is the recipient of an NEA grant for fiction. He teaches at Radford University in Radford, Virginia

www.ingramcontent.com/pod-product-compliance
Lightning Source LLC
Chambersburg PA
CBHW022010080426
42733CB00007B/551